Greenland

through the Year

Karin and Hans Berg

Scroll Press

New York

Greenland is a large island that lies far north in the Atlantic Ocean between America and Europe. Although it is a long way from Europe, Greenland is part of the European country of Denmark.

At the farthest end of one of Greenland's deep fjords lies the little village this story is about. It is built on flat land between the shore of the fjord and the mountains that rise up behind. The people in the village are sheepfarmers. In the wintertime when the snow falls and the cold weather comes, the sheep are kept close to the barns. All winter the sheepfarmers give them food and shelter. But in the spring, the sheepfarmers take the sheep up into the mountains where the grass is green and fresh.

When spring comes, the people in the village work hard from sunrise to sunset. Summer is short in the far north, and there is much work to do to fill the barns with new food before winter comes again. First the fields must be plowed and then planted with seed. Then the crops must be cared for as they grow bigger.

At the end of May, the sheepfarmers herd the sheep together up in the mountains and drive them back to the villages. This job takes many days because the sheep and new lambs have strayed into the mountains far from the village. Some of the sheepfarmers ride horses, while others go on foot. The sheep and their lambs are driven in great flocks across the mountain sides, through the valleys, along lakes and rivers, and down to the village.

Down in the village the flocks of sheep are driven into a big paddock called a sheepfold. The new lambs are marked on their ears with a sign that shows who owns them. The sheeps' wool has grown long over the winter and spring, and it must be sheared. Most of the wool is sent to the market to be sold, but the sheepfarmers' wives keep some to spin into yarn to make warm clothes for the winter. When the shearing is over, the sheep are driven back into the mountains where they spend the summer eating the sweet, green grass.

Soon it is summer, and the grass and grain in the fields is green. Each house has a garden filled with fresh vegetables which the sheepfarmers will store away in their cellars for the long winter.

But summer is short, and soon there is a nip in the air. It is time for the harvest. Everyone helps to bring in the hay and grain at harvest time. It is fun to sit on the top of a load of hay as it goes to the barn!

Before long the ice at the farthest end of the fjord is so thick that the sheepfarmers can walk on it. They cut holes in it and drop their lines down into the water underneath the ice to fish.

When the harvest is over, the sheep must be driven back down from the mountains to the shelter of the village for the winter. Some of the lambs are sold to other villages. They are loaded into barges on the fjord and carried away. It is getting very cold now, and the sheepfarmers must work fast before the fjord freezes and the boats stick fast in the ice.

When the harvest is over, the sheep must be driven back down from the mountains to the shelter of the village for the winter. Some of the lambs are sold to other villages. They are loaded into barges on the fjord and carried away. It is getting very cold now, and the sheepfarmers must work fast before the fjord freezes and the boats stick fast in the ice.

Before long the ice at the farthest end of the fjord is so thick that the sheepfarmers can walk on it. They cut holes in it and drop their lines down into the water underneath the ice to fish.

In winter, the village is almost completely cut off from the rest of Greenland by the ice in the fjords and the wild mountains. But sometimes a ship breaks through the ice and makes its way to the village. Then everyone helps unload the food and goods. Horses are hitched to sleds to carry the goods from the ship to the village.

One morning in the middle of winter, the village woke to find a terrible storm raging. The strong winds lashed the water of the fjord into great waves and snow drifted down from the tops of the mountains. One mighty gust tore a barn roof off. Empty barrels rumbled across the fields.

Winter continued with deep snow and terrible cold. The sheepfarmers had to be careful that the sheep did not stray from the barns in this cold because they would not be able to live. If sheep strayed, the sheepfarmers had to go out into the mountains to rescue them. It was hard to walk in the deep snow, and it was late before the men returned from the mountains with the sheep.

Back in the village, the sheep were driven into the sheepfolds by the stables. The men got hay from the barns to feed them.

Although summer is still far away, the days are getting longer, and there is a smell of spring in the air. Soon the warm sun will shine again, and the sheep will be driven up into the green mountains—and the year in Greenland will start all over again.

First U.S. publication 1973 by Scroll Press, Inc.,
    22 E. 84th St., New York, New York 10028
Copyright © 1972 by Gyldendal, Denmark
Library of Congress No. 72-90689
Printed in the United States of America